Every Tiny Cottage
& Every Little Light
Tell the Secret
of the Trees and of the
Winds at Night

Sarah Janisse Brown

These pages are blank so you can use markers or coloring pens.

Queste pagine sono in bianco in modo da poter utilizzare le penne coloranti.

Ces pages sont vides de sorte que vous pouvez utiliser des stylos à colorier.

Estas páginas están en blanco así que usted puede usar plumas para colorear.

Diese Seiten sind leer, so können Farbstifte verwenden können.

These pages are blank so you can use markers or coloring pens.

Queste pagine sono in bianco in modo da poter utilizzare le penne coloranti.

Ces pages sont vides de sorte que vous pouvez utiliser des stylos à colorier.

Estas páginas están en blanco así que usted puede usar plumas para colorear.

Diese Seiten sind leer, so können Farbstifte verwenden können.

These pages are blank so you can use markers or coloring pens.

Queste pagine sono in bianco in modo da poter utilizzare le penne coloranti.

Ces pages sont vides de sorte que vous pouvez utiliser des stylos à colorier.

Estas páginas están en blanco así que usted puede usar plumas para colorear.

Diese Seiten sind leer, so können Farbstifte verwenden können.

These pages are blank so you can use markers or coloring pens.

Queste pagine sono in bianco in modo da poter utilizzare le penne coloranti.

Ces pages sont vides de sorte que vous pouvez utiliser des stylos à colorier.

Estas páginas están en blanco así que usted puede usar plumas para colorear.

Diese Seiten sind leer, so können Farbstifte verwenden können.

These pages are blank so you can use markers or coloring pens.

Queste pagine sono in bianco in modo da poter utilizzare le penne coloranti.

Ces pages sont vides de sorte que vous pouvez utiliser des stylos à colorier.

Estas páginas están en blanco así que usted puede usar plumas para colorear.

Diese Seiten sind leer, so können Farbstifte verwenden können.

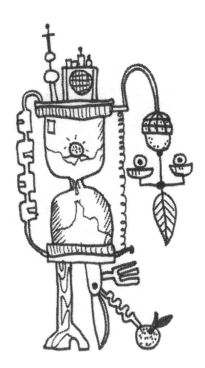

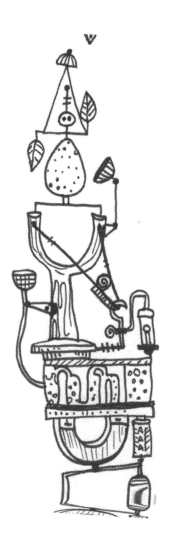

SCIENCE

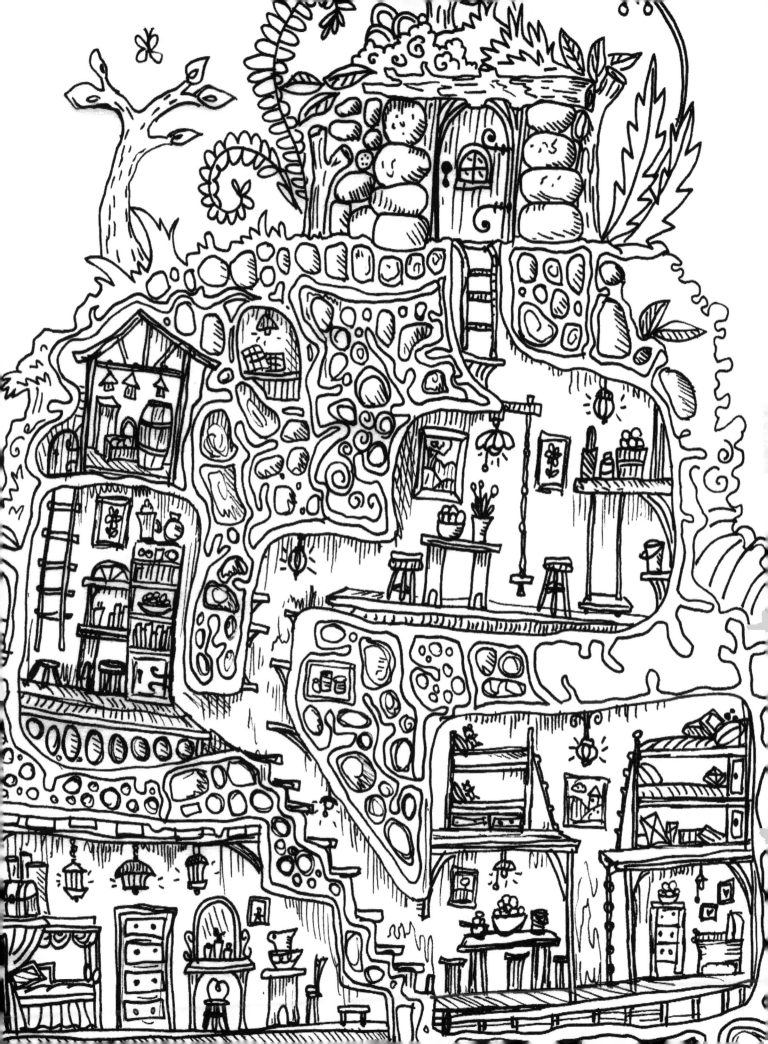

53530058R00059

Made in the USA
Lexington, KY
08 July 2016